WHAT TO DO
WHEN
THE
LIGHTS
GO
OUT

D1157407

by James O. Davis

Cutting Edge International
Orlando, Florida

Unless otherwise indicated, all Scripture quotations are taken from the New American Standard Bible ®. Copyright © The Lockman Foundation 1960, 1962, 1963, 1968, 1971, 1972, 1973, 1975, 1977, 1995. Used by permission.

What to Do When the Lights Go Out

ISBN 1-931682-38-0
Copyright © 2010 James O. Davis

James O. Davis
P. O. Box 411605
Melbourne, FL 32941
www.JamesODavis.org

5-19-14

Angie & Vincent

Heard this speaker at church the other day. Had to buy one for you, me and Jimmy. I truly have believed this way all my life, but sometimes the darkness was too dark! Amazingly, the sun always brought light. How simple a beliefe and how powerful the promise! Read and believe, you will then always have the sun the

In Loving Memory

Our Daughter Jennifer Renee' and Son James Paul

next day!

Love to both

Dad & Mom

CONTENTS

Isaiah 50:3-5, 10, 11

"I clothe the heavens with blackness and make sackcloth their covering. The Lord God has given Me the tongue of disciples that I may know how to sustain the weary one with a word. He awakens Me morning by morning, He awakens My ear to listen as a disciple. The Lord God has opened My ear; and I was not disobedient nor did I turn back. Who is among you that fears the Lord, that obeys the voice of His servant, that walks in darkness and has no light? Let him trust in the Name of the Lord and rely on his God. Behold all you who kindle a fire, who encircle yourselves with firebrands, walk in the light of your fire and among the brands you have set ablaze. This you will have from My hand: you will lie down in torment." (NASB)

DIADEMS OF DARKNESS

Throughout life, we get sick and we get better. But unless the Lord returns in our lifetime, we will all one day get sick and not get better. That's not morbid thinking. It's just mortal reality. None of us is going to live forever on this planet. There is only one way out, and that is through death. We don't like to talk about it, but it's part of living on this earth.

At President Richard Nixon's funeral, Dr. Billy Graham summed it up well when he said, "There is democracy in death. It comes to us equally and makes us equal when it comes."

I was in London in September of 1998, the week that Princess Diana was tragically killed in an automobile accident. I saw the outpouring of roses from around the globe that witnessed to a world mourning the end of her mortal life. But hers was not the only death that I took time to note while in England. It may seem unusual to you, but I have visited a lot of cemeteries as I travel. Like it or not, we will all one day visit a cemetery, so I guess I'm just trying to get used to the idea.

On that particular trip, I visited two cemeteries. One was in the downtown area. It was very small—about the size of an average church sanctuary. I had wanted to go to that cemetery for a long time, for in it were buried the remains of John Bunyan who, in 1672, wrote *Pilgrim's Progress*. *Pilgrim's Progress* is one of the greatest books, outside of the Bible, that has ever been written. I highly recommend it. But when you read *Pilgrim's Progress*, remind yourself that it was not written in the comfort of a living room or from the softness of a sofa. It was written by an incarcerated preacher. John Bunyan was a Puritan preacher who, in the face of conflict with England's Anglican church, would not compromise his gospel position. He wouldn't let the government tell him what he could and could not preach. So they locked him up. It was from the Bedford jail that Bunyan wrote *Pilgrim's Progress*. On one occasion, the warden set a contract outside of John's door with a pencil and said, "Why don't you just sign it, and we will let you go free?"

Bunyan responded, "I will not."

"Then," said the warden, "we will starve your wife. We will starve your daughter. Why don't you just go ahead and sign it?"

Bunyan refused. Under those bleak circumstances, from the cell of a jail, *Pilgrim's Progress* was written.

In that same cemetery, I turned and saw the grave of John Wesley's mother, Susanna. She had seventeen children! One of those children, John became the founder of the Methodist church, helped by his brother, Charles. John Wesley was a man of disciplined faith and uncompromising obedience to the Word of God. More than two hundred years ago, God gave him a vision for the Church. Wesley summed it up by saying, "If a town is big enough for a post office, it is big enough for a church. Let's find out where all the post offices are and put a church right next door." That was Wesley's vision.

Directly across the street from the cemetery stands Wesley's home. I walked across the street, into his house, and up to the second floor. There I stood beside the bed where John Wesley graduated from this earth to eternity. On one side of the bed sat his altar bench with a Bible opened to the place where he had been reading during his last quiet time. As I stood there, I thought, "Here is a man who stayed focused, regardless of what came his way; a visionary leader who understood what it was to walk through darkness."

The second cemetery I visited on that particular trip to England was one of the largest cemeteries in an area outside of London proper. I had to find a driver who could take me there. He asked me whose grave I was going to see. "Charles Haddon Spurgeon," I answered.

"I've never heard of him," he said.

"That doesn't surprise me," I said, "but in the mid-to-late 1800s, there were hundreds of thousands of people, both in London and throughout the world, who listened to the messages of Pastor Spurgeon."

Later, as I stood at the foot of Spurgeon's grave, the words of one of his sermons echoed in my mind: "Small faith will take your soul to heaven, but *great* faith will bring heaven to your soul."

Bunyan, Wesley and Spurgeon were men of great faith. More than the physical proximity they shared in life, faith was their real, eternal bond. Their incredible faith and the fruit of their walks with Christ were the reasons I wanted to see their graves rather than the markers of other famous Englishmen.

It is worthwhile to inquire how they came to such great faith. Was it because God had poured out on them nothing but blessing and ease? Did they come by faith easily because they had known only the goodness of God and not the pain of suffering? Far from it! In fact, quite the opposite. They all discovered secrets of faith and devotion in times as dark as the cell at night time in a Bedford prison.

The secret to great faith is to know how to walk by faith successfully through the darkness until you reach the other side. The central question addressed in this booklet is this: *What do we do when the lights go out?* What do we do when darkness comes our way? I believe that there are treasures in darkness. There are great discoveries to be made about faith during seasons of darkness. There are diadems in the darkness. Some of the greatest lessons of faith we will ever learn are learned during seasons of darkness. This is the essential truth that I want to communicate in these few pages. If you let Him, God will write this message on your heart so that you will never forget it.

Here are the diadems of darkness:

- The Devotion of Faith: *Those of Deepest Devotion Know The Deepest Darkness*
- The Development of Faith: *The Faith That Is Born In The Light Is Developed In The Dark*
- The Discernment of Faith: *There Are Some Things You Can See In The Dark That You Cannot See In The Light*
- The Danger of Faith: *It Is Better To Serve God In Darkness Than To Stand Alone In Self-made Light*
- The Daybreak of Faith: *If Your Sun Has Gone Down, It Will Come Back Up Again*

THE DEVOTION OF FAITH:
Those of Deepest Devotion Know The
Deepest Darkness

There is a wrong-headed belief that is subconsciously held by many believers. Upon examination, we can recognize its falsehood. But something inside of us wants to believe that people of deep devotion will not walk through difficulty; that their great faith will afford them some special exemption from hardship and suffering. Scripture, as well as experience, tells us that nothing is further from the truth. On the contrary, there are people in the world who will lose their lives not for lack of faith, but because they had so much of it. You may have heard of people on the leading edge, but there are also people on the *bleeding* edge. Do you know that there are more people being killed by martyrdom in the present era than at any other time in the history of the Church? They are being martyred not because they lack faith, but because they have enough faith to stay faithful to the end.

The life of Job is the classic illustration of deep devotion and deep darkness. In Job 19:8, we read, "God put darkness in Job's path." Yet God loved Job and Job loved God! There was no chasm between Job and God, no broken relationship that caused God to abandon him to suffering. Indeed, by the end of the story, Job said that through his trials his faith became like pure gold. It is true that at the end of Job's story, the Lord doubled everything that he had lost, but it was in deep darkness that Job's faith and devotion were tested. What about you? While walking through such losses, can you still trust the Lord's Word and promises? Even when your family and friends laugh at you or tell you to give up?

If it has been awhile since you have read the book of Habakkuk, it is a great book to read, especially given today's challenging times. It only takes about fifteen minutes to read the whole book. In chapter one, Habakkuk starts asking God big questions. It's okay to ask God big questions! He can handle it.

Habakkuk asked God, "Are you paying attention to what is going on down here? When are you going to put a stop to all of this injustice?" Have you ever wondered that? Have you ever wondered when God is going to put an end to injustice? One day, He will.

Habakkuk continues questioning God, saying, "Do you see the unrighteous prospering and the righteous suffering? Would you please tell me what in the world is going on?"

God gave Habakkuk an answer: "If I were to tell you, you would not be able to understand it." Sometimes, God's answer is that He is doing something bigger than us. When that's His answer, we need simply to accept it.

Yet, Habakkuk continues to push forward by telling the Lord that he is quite capable of understanding his times. So God answers him, "I am going to raise up the Babylonians and they are going to take the Israelites into captivity."

Habakkuk was expecting a much different answer. He was thinking that God was going to reverse injustice and put a stop to the sin affecting His people. But it gets even worse. If Habakkuk thought the "morning newspaper" was filled with bad news, the "evening news" was even more disappointing. Nonetheless, we don't find Habakkuk wallowing in despair. He doesn't abandon his faith in God because the lights are going dim in Israel. In fact, by the end of chapter three, Habakkuk is praising God, saying, "I've got hinds' feet in high places. I've learned how to rejoice."

Habakkuk literally sings, "Though there be no cattle in the field, though the crops are all gone, yet I will rejoice in the Lord."

How was Habakkuk able to rejoice in the face of bad news? How was he able to go from low to high? How was he able to make that transition? The answer is found in Habakkuk 2:1: "The just shall live by faith." I'm glad that Habakkuk said that, because centuries later, the Apostle Paul was able to rephrase it in his famous declaration, "The righteous shall live by faith." (Rom. 1;17; Gal. 3;11) Habakkuk said it first. Years later, Martin Luther echoed it yet again.

What about us? What about our dark days? How do we live in days like ours as Habakkuk did in his unjust and disappointing era? We *still* live by faith! "The just shall live by faith." Our faith is not in man. Our faith is in God.

If you want faith, put your faith in the right place. If you only have faith in yourself, then you'll get what you alone can bring about. If you put your faith in your family, you will get only what your family can accomplish. That won't be enough. If you put your faith in your organization, then you will get only what your organization can do. This still will not be enough. If we want great faith, we put our faith in a great God. When we put our faith in God, He can move heaven and earth to give us victory in this world for His glory.

Victory is greatest when it overcomes great odds. The Glory of God shines brightest against the backdrop of the deepest darkness. Those with the deepest faith and devotion are often those who have gone through the deepest darkness.

In the New Testament, the classic example of this first diadem of darkness is John the Baptist. From the darkness of a dungeon cell he sent the first century equivalent of an e-mail to the Messiah, asking him, "Are you the one who was to come, or should we look for somebody else?" Imagine that! The long foretold forerunner of the Anointed One is questioning the very essence of who Jesus is.

The Lord replied, saying "The blind see, the deaf hear, and the lame walk. I am who I said I am."

Some may criticize John the Baptist. After all, should he have even been questioning the very core of the character of the Messiah? But before we are too hard on him, do you recall what Jesus Christ once said about John the Baptist? He said, "… among those born of women there is no one greater than John." (Lk. 7:28) How would you like an asterisk like at the bottom of your resume that said, "No one born has ever been greater." That's who John the Baptist was!

The point is, John's place was not diminished because his personal darkness caused him to question God. He was still the *greatest* in Jesus' eyes. He died a man of remarkable faith and unyielding belief in Jesus the Messiah. That's comforting! That's great news! When periods of darkness overshadow our lives and we ask foundational questions about God and what He's up to, we are in the greatest of company. Those of deepest devotion have often gone through the deepest darkness.

Read church history and you will find that all Christian men and women of renowned faith, if they lived long enough, went through the "midnight hour" or "dark night of the soul." Indeed, whether one studies historic mystics like St. John of the Cross and Theresa of Avila or contemporary Christian guides like Dallas Willard, Richard Foster, Eugene Peterson, and Janet Hagberg, they all mention the school of faith that comes with brokenness before God.

Our world throws away broken things, but God uses broken things. One of the great paradoxes of the Christian spiritual life is that wholeness in Christ is only reached through the portal of brokenness.

The same week that Princess Di passed away, Mother Theresa of Calcutta also passed away. Compared to the worldwide outpouring of grief that accompanied the death of the princess, there wasn't much fanfare surrounding Mother Theresa's death. But that probably suited her just fine. For, before her death, she made this statement: "You will never know that Jesus is all you need, until all you have is Jesus." You and I may mentally assent to that statement, but she lived it. When Mother Theresa died, she had to her name a bucket, a stick, and a pair of worn-out sandals. She could claim more than intellectual assent to the all-sufficiency of Jesus. Her life proved that she believed it.

Jesus Christ is not just *an* answer; Jesus Christ is *the* answer. Jesus said, "I am the way and the truth." Truth is a person. Truth is not a concept that we reason with. Truth is embodied in a person with whom we can have a relationship. To survive the midnight hours of the soul, to emerge from the darkness, is to trust even in dark times the all-sufficient reality of Jesus. Jesus is as real as the pew you sit in on Sunday morning. He alone will take you through the darkness to the other side for the Glory of God. Those with the deepest devotion have often gone through the deepest darkness.

THE DEVELOPMENT OF FAITH
The Faith That Is Born In The Light Is Developed In The Dark

Faith is like film. It is developed in the dark.

I get a lot of phone calls, but let me tell you about the phone calls I *don't* get. I don't get calls from friends saying, "Hey James, I just wanted to call and let you know that everything is wonderful! Will you fast with me in prayer?" Do *you* get those calls? Of course not! The calls I get are often from people who say, "Things not going so well. Would you please agree with me in prayer?"

We grow more during times of challenge than at any other times in our lives. Isn't it the case that the prayer closet is used more during times of sickness than in times of health? And when is the Bible most often read? In times of prosperity or during times of financial trouble? When you read the Bible, the Bible reads you. It's not like TIME Magazine. It's not like some other book. It is the living breathing Word of God that bathes your soul, illumines your mind and fills your spirit as you read.

Today it is hard to have a quiet time. Ironically, there are some people in our churches who get upset that there is no prayer in school, but they are not upset when there is no prayer in their own home! Prayer starts in the homes of the people of Almighty God.

Regarding a quiet time, it is a time for devotion, and it is a time of "quiet." Every person can listen better when we're not talking. Even if your traditions are loud prayer times, it is still okay to be quiet sometimes. During my quiet time, I spend more time *not* saying anything.

If you read any of the classics on Christian formation, you will find commended over and over again the practice of being silent before God. After all, what we have to say is kind of small compared to what He has to say. We need the kind of faith that believes that what He has to say to me is more important than what I have to say to Him, especially since He already knows everything that is in my mind and on my heart. I want to hear what He might say to me. For each of us, we need to let our "quiet times" be quiet sometimes.

You may say, "Well, I have my quiet time on my way to work." You may try to do that, but just remember the other name for that time of day, which is, "rush hour!" It is most often anything but quiet!

What about listening to God's Word? Do you believe everything you read in the newspaper? I don't. I hope you don't either. Do you believe everything you read in the Bible? I do. I hope you do, too. But here's the question we have to ask ourselves: Do we spend more time reading what we don't believe than what we do believe? If so, why?

Think about it! We get a good night's sleep and then wake up and read bad news. We read up on the North Koreans being bad, the stock market being down, the team losing, and the crime committed. Why do we choose to start our day like that? Many people will get up from a good sleep, on a good day, grab a good breakfast, then sit down to watch bad news.

How much better and more profitable to start our day before the throne of God, quietly listening for God's voice and reading God's Word. That's how our faith is developed every day of our lives, whether that day is light and bright or deep and dark. Faith that is born in the light is developed in the dark. A pastor may bring a message on a given Sunday that causes "the lights to go on," but *between* Sundays, we may have to walk through the darkness. Every day, we need take in some of the light of God's Word and be enlightened by the voice of God heard in prayer.

I have had the same amazing experience in this mortal life many times that lends insight into what happens in the spiritual life. You probably have, too. It is this: I am able to get up in the middle of the night, when all of the lights are off, and find the refrigerator. In the dark! Without turning on a light! It's absolutely amazing! I stun myself. How about you? Can you find the refrigerator at night? I'll bet you can.

How do we do that? Well, how did we learn where the refrigerator was in the first place? We learned during the daytime, when it was light. In the light, we learned where the bedroom door was, where the kitchen table was, where the counter was. When the lights are out, we are able to tip-toe through the house, find the kitchen, then the refrigerator and the hidden treasures within it. We learned in the light what to do in the dark!

Likewise, the Lord teaches us how to walk by faith in the light so that we might successfully walk by faith in the dark. That's why it is important that we immerse ourselves in the Word of God. The Word of God is a light. It is a treasure. It is a road map to help us walk successfully in this world. It is important to approach God in prayer and soak in God's Word. It's also important to have prayer partners, so that we may agree together in prayer and agree with one another in spirit. Once we have these things in the light, we are more apt to be successful when the lights go out. Faith that was born in the light is developed in the dark.

The great Bible teacher Warren Wiersbe stated, "We don't live by explanations; we live by God's promises." There is wisdom in that statement. Think about how much you don't understand, or how much you can't explain. We don't live our lives by explanation alone. We live by God's promises. If we only live according to whether we understand something, we will be "up" when we understand and "down" when we don't. We will be like a termite in a yo-yo. Life won't make sense if we only believe what we can see.

Some people say that they discern God's will based upon circumstances. It could be true sometimes, or circumstances could reinforce what we already believe God is doing in our lives, but as a general rule of practice, trusting in circumstances is not wise at all. If you make decisions based only on circumstances, then when circumstances don't make sense, you will be confused. You may conclude that God is not good. We don't live by explanations or by circumstances. We live by God's promises. We walk by God's promises whether we are surrounded by light or by darkness. God's promises are always consistent, always the same.

People who live by circumstances say things like, "under the circumstances," they will do something. Who wants to live underneath circumstances? That's like getting into bed to throw the covers over your head and sleeping underneath the mattress instead.

In the same way, some people make a conscious decision, and a bad decision, not to live on the promises of God. They say, "I'm going to live on what I can understand, under the circumstances." They will suffocate down there, just like a man under his mattress. God has not called us to live "under the circumstances." We are called to live on the promises of Almighty God. One will suffocate us; the other will give us access to the life-giving breath of God.

There are also Christians whose faith is like a roller coaster…up and down and all around. That's not the way God has called us to live our lives. He has called us to live on His promises. If we won't consistently rely on God's promises for our own sakes, then perhaps we could be motivated to do it for the sake of others. People are watching us, especially in days like these. They are watching to see whether we live by newspaper explanations and circumstances or by God's promises.

We are to base our lives clearly and succinctly on the Word of God. Where reason cannot wade, faith will swim. That doesn't mean that we don't take out the tape measure now and then, or pick up the computer and calculate certain things. We don't abandon reason. Jesus said, "Wise is the person who counts the cost before he or she builds the house." There are times, however, when God will ask us to do something that is beyond our reasoning ability. There are times when God will ask us to take a step of faith before we have it all figured out. He calls us to be obedient and take a step of faith. Once we take that step, God will reveal more to us. Old maps will not work in new lands. As God brings us into a new territory, God gives us a new map.

There are still other people who believe that they should live on God's promises, regardless of the circumstances. When people live above the circumstance, and live on the promises of God, they don't tithe only when the stock market is up. They just tithe, regardless of circumstances. They don't tithe just when the GNP is going up, or a raise is due or profits are going up. They tithe because God tells us to tithe. People who live on God's promises don't just come to God in prayer during times of difficulty. They come to God in prayer every day. We can live a consistent Christian life because we have great faith in a great God. Christians who base their lives on God's promises are the most consistent people in the world.

I wish you could meet a wonderful brother and friend of mine, Suliasi Kurulo, who pastors a church in Suva, Fiji. Fiji is the 163rd poorest nation in the world. He started the church, the World Harvest Centre, in 1991 in the midst of persecution. He started it with the world in mind. Out of 22 island nations, the World Harvest Centre is now the strongest church in all of Oceania. But to reach that bright place, pastor Kurulo had to walk through darkness, including the death of his oldest son. Not only that, but he was also forced to walk through deep persecution, not at the hands of a hostile secular government, but worse, at the hands of the "old guard," an old main-line group that wanted to keep things the old way.

One night, he walked out into a starry night, looked up into the sky and listened in quietness. God said to him, "Look at these stars. This is what your harvest is going to be like. I'm going to use you to take the gospel around the world." Suliasi Kurulo is now fifty-one years old, and over the last twelve years the church in Suva has planted more than 1100 churches in more than 100 nations around the world. They are sending missionaries out of that impoverished little island nation to places that have never heard the gospel! Pastor Kurulo believed that God asked him to do that. He walked by faith and so it was done!

Faith that is born in the light is developed in the dark. It is not reasonable to believe that a Fijian leader in the South Pacific could send gospel missionaries to over one hundred nations without any source of income but their own impoverished church people. But they began to take steps of faith and God began to bless. God continued to pour out in marvelous ways. That congregation now makes up one of the greatest missionary-sending churches in all the world.

Sometimes, God will ask us to do something that, in the natural realm, we can't get our minds around.

But, once we take that step of faith, God will show us more steps of obedience to cooperate with the divine plan, accomplishing the will of God. Sometimes those with the deepest devotion experience the deepest darkness. Faith that is born in the light is developed in the dark.

THE DISCERNMENT OF FAITH
There Are Some Things You Can See In The Dark
That You Cannot See In The Light

The Milky Way galaxy where we live, is about six trillion miles wide. That is about the distance that light travels in a year. If you were to count the stars in the Milky Way at the rate of one star per second, it would take 2500 years to count them all. And those are just the stars in *our* galaxy. Astrophysicists tell us that there are five hundred billion galaxies in the universe. Each of those contains at least one hundred billion stars.

When I drive through places like northern Arizona at night, away from the lights of any city, I like to stop. I enjoy getting out of the car and feasting my eyes on the twinkling heavens above. The darker it is, the better the stars can be seen. Why are there so many stars? The Bible says that the stars declare the greatness of God, to declare the praise of God. But, we wouldn't have a single star by which to praise God if we didn't have the backdrop of darkness against which the stars stand out. Likewise, we wouldn't understand the diadems of faith were it not for dark times.

There are some things you can see in the dark that you cannot see in the light. On a beautiful day when the sun is out, we can't see the stars. In the daytime, we see things that are "near," but at night we see things much further away; billions of miles away. In the daytime we can learn things about ourselves, but against the backdrop of darkness, we learn things about God.

It is amazing how quickly people can reprioritize their lives when darkness comes. A healthy man shrugs when the doctor advises him to take his vitamins every day. He protests, "But I feel good, doctor!" Six months later, feeling weak and ill, he tries to take six months worth of vitamins in one afternoon to make up for his negligence and wonders why it doesn't restore him.

We can't restore our health by "cramming." Physical health isn't developed in an instant; it is the cumulative effect of a healthy lifestyle consistently lived over time. People who have good health have maintained healthy practices when they felt like it and when they didn't. Likewise, the follower of Christ who is strong in faith has practiced a consistent diet of prayer and reliance upon God's promises, both in good times and in dark times.

There are some things you can see in the dark that you cannot see in the light!

When we walk by faith in the midst of the night, we can see how great our God is. God knows all the names of the stars and He knows how to number them. God knows every hair on our heads and every blade of grass on the earth and every drop of water that falls from the sky. He knows everything there is about this universe and he knows everything there is to know about you and about me.

When the darkness comes, do you know what time it is? It is time to learn more about the King of the universe. It is time to take a look at the stars and realize how great, how grand, how glorious is our Lord. It is time to recognize that He is so big and we are so small. It is in times of darkness that we most grow and mature. We become bigger people. Those with the deepest devotion have often known the deepest darkness. There are some things you can see in the dark that you just can't see in the light.

THE DANGER OF FAITH
It Is Better To Serve God In Darkness Than To Stand Alone In Self-made Light

I have two beautiful daughters. When they were young, they did not like the dark. When I would tuck them in at night, they would say, "Daddy, will you please leave a light on?" If the door accidentally closed, I would hear, "Daddy!" Immediately, I would know what the problem is. It's dark.

Most Christians don't like the dark, either. As soon as darkness comes, we do our best to get the lights back on. Darkness never overcomes the light. Light always overcomes the darkness. Darkness flees from light.

When we stand near the front door of our home at night, we can turn on the inside lights, then open up the front door and invite darkness in. We can call to it, "Come inside, darkness. Come on in!" But, darkness will not tread where light has taken up residence. Darkness cannot displace light. Yet, if you turn off the interior light, the darkness that was outside will rush inside.

You can tell a lot about people by watching how they respond to darkness in their lives. Watch how people respond when a challenge comes their way. Watch what happens when there is downsizing at work. People will gossip at the water fountain. They will jostle for position because they don't like the darkness. Watch when darkness comes to a family. Watch the struggle and civil war that breaks out. People don't like darkness. But darkness exposes what is within us, whether it be the sweetness of light or the bitterness of darkness. Like a toothpaste tube emits toothpaste when squeezed, whatever is inside of people will come out when pressure is applied. Listen to what people say and you'll find out what is inside their hearts.

Jesus said, "Out of the overflow of the heart, the mouth speaks." (Mt. 12:34)

I told my oldest daughter, "Olivia, always stay sweet." She said, "Why is that daddy?" I said, "Because, then, when life squeezes you, sweetness will come out."

If we don't have sweetness inside, then sourness will come out when challenges come our way. People don't like to hang around sour people. People don't like hanging around people who have a sour spirit or harbor bitterness in their hearts. God wills that we be filled with better things from Him.

Abraham was called "the Father of the Faithful." When we study his life in the early chapters of Genesis, we find that he would build an altar, dig a well, build an altar, dig a well. That is, he would take care of the spiritual, then the physical. First was always the spiritual, then the physical. Except on one occasion. Darkness came to Father Abraham in the form of a famine in Genesis 18 and 19. In that time of darkness, Abraham did not ask if it was okay to go to Egypt. He did not pray about it. Absolutely not. God didn't say a word to him that it was okay to go to Egypt. What did Abraham do? He packed up his wife and their belongings and they went down to Egypt.

It was in this time of darkness, when Abraham wasn't walking by the light of God, that he met Hagar. It was in this darkness, that Hagar birthed his illegitimate son Ishmael. Ishmael was born "of the flesh," not "of the promise" of God. Isaac was born according to the promise. Ishmael came out of the circumstances. Isaac came out of the promise.

The works of the flesh acted against the promises of God. Much suffering has come to the world because Abraham did not wait on God. The works of the flesh will act against the promises of God in your life as well. How we handle darkness impacts those who follow us.

Time spent waiting on God is not time wasted. Some people try to manipulate the darkness, impatiently forcing a lesson that is not the one God would teach. They try to make darkness mean something that it doesn't really mean. They are like the man who got up at half-past-midnight and went outside with his flashlight to look at the sun dial. He could make it say any time he wanted it to say! Wise is the person who does not manipulate the darkness nor create his own version of light, but waits for God to turn on the light and teach what He wills.

If God has allowed darkness to come into our lives, wise are we as Christians to wait on God to shine the light that delivers us. Let us not be one who picks up our own flashlight to make the darkness say what we want it to say. It is better to serve God in darkness than to stand alone in self-made light.

THE DAYBREAK OF FAITH
If Your Sun Has Gone Down, It Will Come Back Up Again

We may weep for the night, but joy comes in the morning. The sun may have gone down, but it isn't going to stay down.

Just as the seed goes into the ground to die, but comes back up again as a tree, so will the sun will come back up. We just give it time. God is not finished with us. He is molding and shaping us to become more like His Son. God's goal is not to make us happy. His ultimate goal is not even to make us healthy. His number one goal is to make us holy, to make us more like Jesus Christ. Does He want us to be happy? Yes, He does. The joy of the Lord is our strength. Does He want us to be healthy? Of course He does. But His first priority is to transform us; to make us more like Jesus Christ.

In the 23rd Psalm, we read these words: "Though I walk through the valley of the shadow of death, I will fear no evil. For my God is with me." Read them aloud and really hear them!

Listen again to what David the Psalmist wrote! "Though I walk through the valley of the shadow..." Consider this: If there is a "shadow" of darkness in our lives, it means that there is light shining down upon us. There is only one way that a shadow can exist around us...we must have a light shining upon us.

In the spirit life, a "shadow" in our lives reminds us that God's light is shining upon us. If we didn't have a light shining upon us, we wouldn't have a shadow. Instead, we'd have complete darkness. The shadows remind us that God's light is shining upon us.

Listen to how David continues: "Though I walk through the valley of the shadow *of death*..." The psalm describes *death* as a shadow. Sometimes shadows can frighten us even though they cannot hurt us. Sometimes death will frighten us, but death cannot hurt us. Death is only a shadow.

If there is a "shadow" of darkness in our lives, it means that there is light shining down upon us!

In the "valley of the shadow of death" David wrote, "I will fear no evil..." The Valley of the Shadow of Death was an actual place. It was a dreadful, intimidating place through which one must travel on the road up to Jerusalem from Jericho. It was a place favored by thieves and murderers who took advantage of travelers that braved a road adjacent to deadly terrain. Many lost their belongings or even their lives there. So, how is it that David could say that he was not afraid while walking through such a valley?

First, David knew *who* he was.

Secondly, David knew *where* he was. Where was he? In a valley. But what's a valley? A valley is a low place between two high places. In order to have a valley, there must be mountains on either side. If there are not mountains on the left and on the right, then we don't have a valley! David may have been walking through the valley of the shadow of death, but he knew that he had mountains on his left and on his right.

In fact, Psalm 23 itself is what we call a "valley psalm." That is, the psalm itself is actually nestled between two mighty mountains. In Psalm 22 is mount Calvary. In Psalm 24 is mount Zion. In Psalm 23, there is the valley. In Psalm 22 is the blood-drenched mountain called Calvary. In Psalm 24 is the snow capped mountain of Zion. In Psalm 22, the mount represents Jesus' first coming. In Psalm 24, the mount represents his second coming. Psalm 22 is his death. Psalm 24 is his reign.

Where do we walk? We walk through the valley of the shadow of death. But there are shadows because God's light is shining down on us, and it is a valley because there are mountains on our left and on our right. We look to the left and we see where Jesus Christ died for us. We look to the right and we see where Jesus Christ is coming back for us. We look to the left and we see our past paid for. We look to the right and we see our future where we will reign with Christ.

While we are walking through the valley of the shadow of death, we fear no evil, for God is with us!

One day we will come out on the other side. When we do, there will be no more darkness. There will be no more fear and death and dread. Never again! That is the plan God has for us. The Lord never promised us smooth sailing. But, He promised us a safe landing. He didn't say that it wouldn't get rough. He said it would turn out alright at the end. One day, we are going to stand on the seashore of eternity and enter into what the Bible describes as "the joy of the Lord." If your sun has gone down, it will come back up again.

After experiencing a long valley in my life, there came a day that I will never forget. I was standing in the kitchen of our home in Springfield, Missouri, on February 9th when my cell phone rang. I answered and a lady on the other side asked, "Is this James

Davis?" I said, "Yes." She said, "I manage security at the White House."

I said, "Ma'am, I didn't do it. I promise you, I have an identical twin brother. My parents didn't have a creative bone in their bodies, so when my brother was born sixteen minutes after me, they just called him James, too. So, whatever this is about, it wasn't me, it was my twin."

She chuckled for a second and then said, "Your name is on a list of about fifty people invited to have breakfast with the President in the morning."

I said, "I don't know why I am on that list; I am honored to be invited, but I won't be able to attend. My wife and I are going to mainland China to adopt our first baby girl, Olivia, whom God created before the foundation of the world. You understand, this is a pretty big thing. If you don't mind, could you relay that to our President? I would be honored to be there, but I promised my wife that we would go shopping tonight to buy what we need to be ready for our daughter. If I'm on a plane going to the White House, then I won't be able to keep my word. You have to understand, this is a huge thing for the Davis family. Thank you, and goodbye."

When I hung up, my wife's eyes were as big as saucers. She said, "You're really not going?" I said, "We can go to the White House any day. We're going to China to adopt our baby girl, so let's get ready!"

Our family pictures include little Olivia, our oldest, and then Priscilla the youngest, both made in China. My wife, Sheri, and I lost two children, James and Jennifer, in the 90s. If you were to ask me whether I would have back James and Jennifer, but that I would have to exchange Olivia and Priscilla, I would not make that deal. It's not that I did not love James and Jennifer. And it's not that I love Olivia and Priscilla more. But, if my wife and I hadn't walked through the graveyard of the heart-wrenching loss of our children, we wouldn't have made it to China. We wouldn't have known the brightness that Olivia and Priscilla brought into our lives and they might never have known life outside of an orphanage.

Did Sheri and I sin, and that's why we lost our children? Did we have a lack of faith that displeased God? Of course not! When you are walking through darkness, it does not mean that you have sinned. It does not mean that God is put out with you. It just means that God knows how to make you a better Christian.

We give God time to put the pieces of our lives together. When He does, we will look back and say, "I'm so much larger in my spirit than I was before." We learn things about God that we didn't know. We come to the conclusion that our God is awesome and great and glorious. No matter where we are when we started, God knows how to get us through the darkness and to the other side.

I do not speak out of my head knowledge, but out of my heart. Many people are in darkness today. Taking steps in the night may frighten them. They may be worried and anxious, wondering if the sun will ever come up again. They may say, "O God, will you make this stop and give me Your light again"?" They may feel alone. They may feel that even people whom they knew very well no longer understand how they feel. And the truth is, maybe those people don't. But, God does!

God is touched with the very feelings of our infirmities. He is concerned about us even more than we are concerned about ourselves. Though our God is the Creator of the Universe—some 500 billion plus galaxies—He sees us right where we are.

You, where you sit right now, are the highest form of God's creation. He looks at you and sees every aspect of your life. He is concerned about you. He is asking you to trust Him until the sun comes up.

The Bible says, "... rely upon your God." This means waiting until the sun comes up. He knows exactly what you are going through and He knows how to get you through it. He knows how to take care of the cares of your life. Place your burden upon the Lord's shoulders. Let Him carry it from this day forward. Trust and rely upon Him to take care of whatever you are facing. For the light shines in the darkness and the darkness has not overcome it. Indeed, the backdrop of darkness makes the Glory of God shine all the brighter. Walk in the dark as you learned to walk in the light and walk the same way, depending on the promises, despite all circumstances, even when the lights go out.

THE TREASURE MAP
Five Spiritual Steps to the Sunshine

The following exercises are offered as a pathway through the darkness; a treasure map, as it were, to discovering the diadems of faith that can only be found when the lights go out. The exercises are neither shallow nor short, but then, neither is your suffering. You deserve the full breadth and depth of help that is available.

1. Devotion of Faith

   Have you ever loved the Lord more in the past than you do now?

   _____

   _____

   _____

   _____

   _____

   Is there any sin or stronghold that has caused a chasm between the Lord and you?

   _____

   _____

   _____

   _____

   What are the top three areas in which you recognize a need for growth during this time of darkness?

   _____

   _____

   _____

Read and study the books of Job and Habakkuk, and the story of John the Baptist.

Establish three prayer partners until "the sun rises again." Write down their names here, along with their contact information.

_____

_____

_____

Read *Pilgrim's Progress*, written by John Bunyan.

2. The Development of Faith

Select five Bible promises that relate to your situation. Commit them to memory.

1. _____

2. _____

3. _____

4. _____

5. _____

Read Dr. Elmer Towns' book, entitled, *Fasting For Spiritual Breakthrough*.

What fast best relates to your situation?

_____

_____

_____

_____

_____

_____

_____

_____

Continue to agree in prayer with your partners. What have your prayer partners taught you?

_____

_____

_____

Evaluate where you are in your spiritual journey and write down where you want to be in twelve months. Write down a 100-word description of where you are and another 100-word description of where you want to be.

_____

_____

_____

_____

_____

_____

_____

_____

_____

_____

_____

_____

3. **The Discernment of Faith**

Read and study the scriptures that relate how the universe declares the glory and greatness of God. Take a late-night walk, away from any lights, and gaze upon the stars.

Write a description of what you learn during the daytime, compared to what you learn in the night. For example, what do you learn at work during the day?

_____

_____

_____

_____

_____

_____

_____

_____

_____

_____

_____

What do you learn when you are facing the sickness of someone else?

_____

_____

_____

_____

_____

_____

_____

Read E. M. Bounds' book entitled *E.M. Bounds on Prayer.*

What are the top lessons you learned?

_____

_____

_____

_____

_____

_____

_____

4. The Danger of Faith

What are the top five things that frighten you? How well are you handling theses fears?

1. _____

2. _____

3. _____

4. _____

5. _____

Are you sleeping well at night, or are you fearful? If you are afraid, describe your fears at night.

_____

_____

_____

_____

_____

_____

_____

_____

_____

Are your prayer partners staying in consistent contact with you, and you with them? Do you need to replace a prayer partner with someone more faithful?

_____

_____

_____

_____

_____

Are you manipulating the darkness? Are you trying to create your own light?

_____

_____

_____

If so, pin-point the way(s) that you are trying to do so and eliminate it/them.

_____

_____

_____

Read and study the life of Abraham in Genesis 18—22 and in Galatians chapters 4 and 5.

5. The Daybreak of Faith

How long has it been dark? Do you believe that the sun is about to come up in your life? If not, why not?

_____

_____

_____

_____

_____

_____

How will you know that "the sun has risen again?"

_____

_____

_____

_____

_____

_____

What did you learn during the darkness?

_____

_____

_____

_____

_____

_____

What priorities did you change during this dark
period?

_____

_____

_____

_____

_____

_____

_____

_____

ABOUT THE AUTHOR

Dr. James O. Davis founded Cutting Edge International and co-founded the Billion Soul Network, a growing coalition of more than 750 Christian ministries and denominations synergizing their efforts to build the premier community of pastors worldwide to help plant five million new churches for a billion soul harvest. The Billion Soul Network, with more than 200,000 churches, has become the largest pastors network in the world.

Christian leaders recognize Dr. Davis as one of the leading networkers in the Christian world. More than 40,000 pastors and leaders have attended his biannual pastors conference and leadership summits across the US and in all major world regions. During 2007-2009, leaders committed to plant more than three million new churches. He has networked with significant leaders from different spheres such as George O. Wood, Jack Hayford, Johnny Hunt, Robert Schuller, D. James Kennedy, Reinhard Bonnke, Chuck Norris, Charles Blake, Barry Black and others.

Dr. Davis served twelve years leading 1500 evangelists and training thousands of students for full-time evangelism as the National Evangelists Representative at the Assemblies of God world headquarters. Ministering more than 45 weeks per year for 25 years to an average yearly audience of 100,000 people, Dr. Davis has now traveled nearly seven million miles to minister face-to-face to more than 5,000,000 people in nearly 100 nations.

Dr. Davis earned a Doctorate in Ministry in Preaching at Trinity Evangelical Divinity School and two master's degrees from the Assemblies of God Theological Seminary. As an author and editor, he has provided: *The Pastor's Best Friend; The New Testament Evangelist; Living Like Jesus; The Preacher's Summit; Gutenberg to Google: The Twenty Indispensable Laws of Communication*. He co-authored with Dr. Bill Bright, *Beyond All Limits: The Synergistic Church for a Planet in Crisis*. His quotes and articles have appeared in Charisma, Ministry Today, The Challenge Weekly, New York Times Magazine, and elsewhere.

Dr. Davis resides in the Orlando area with his wife, Sheri, and daughters, Olivia and Priscilla. They have two children, Jennifer and James, who reside in heaven.

James O. Davis
P. O. Box 411605
Melbourne, Florida 32941-1605
(417) 861-9999
www.JamesODavis.org

More dynamic books
by Dr. James O. Davis

The Pastor's Best Friend

Living Like Jesus

Gutenberg to Google: The Twenty Indispensable Laws of Communication

Sign Posts To Armageddon

Beyond All Limits: The Synergistic Church For A Planet In Crisis

If this book has ministered to you, please prayerfully consider giving monthly support to Cutting Edge International at www.JamesODavis.org. Those who provide monthly support receive a FREE copy of each new book that Dr. Davis releases.